The Silly Little Book

of

PRACTICAL JOKES

The Silly Little Book of

PRACTICAL

JOKES

EDITED BY ESTHER SELSDON

This is a Parragon Book first published 2000

Parragon
Queen Street House
4 Queen Street
Bath BA1 1HE

Copyright © Parragon 2000

Produced by Magpie Books, an imprint of
Robinson Publishing Ltd, London

ISBN 0 75253 482 3

A copy of the British Library Cataloguing-in-Publication Data
is available from the British Library

Printed and bound in Singapore

Contents

Introduction

A practical joke is a harmless moment of fun to be played on anyone that you know who has a sense of humor and won't get hurt. Remember that if it makes your "victim" cry or ache, it just wasn't funny. Bearing that simple lesson in mind – have fun and get pranking.

At Home

Equipment: Paint and paper.
Joke: Paint some fake eyes on your chin and then hang upside down over the arm of the sofa and scare your mother.

You: What do you call a noisy football fan?
Dad: I give up.
You: A foot-bawler.

Equipment: Today's and yesterday's newspapers.

Joke: Take the cover page of today's newspaper and insert the rest of yesterday's inside. Your parents will happily read for hours and never notice.

You: What's furry and crunchy and needs extra milk?

Mom: I give up.

You: Mice Crispies.

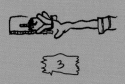

Equipment: A camera with no film in it.

Joke: Go round the house taking pretend photos of your family at embarrassing moments. When they complain, say you'll sell them back for chocolates.

You: What kind of ant likes maths?
Dad: I give up.
You: An account-ant.

Equipment: Lots of small pieces of metal.

Joke: Offer to do the washing up for your mother and, as soon as she's left the kitchen, drop all the pieces of metal onto the floor with a loud clang.

You: Where do you find exploding soup?

Mom: I give up.

You: At the Minestrone of Defense.

Equipment: A chest of drawers.
Joke: Carefully empty the top drawer of your mother's chest and store the contents. Then put the drawer back in the wrong way up.

You: What happened to the apple tart who got arrested?
Dad: I give up.
You: It was remanded in custardy.

Equipment: Some bathroom scales.

Joke: Alter the dial on the scales just before your sister gets on so that she now weighs fifteen stone.

You: What do Italian ghosts eat for dinner?

Mom: I give up.

You: Spookhetti.

Equipment: A baby brother.
Joke: Ask your brother if he's ever seen a man-eating fish. Then take him into the kitchen to watch your Dad eating his cod and fries.

You: What lies at the bottom of the sea shaking violently?
Dad: I give up.
You: A nervous wreck.

Equipment: A door bell.
Joke: Wait until your mother has just got into the bath and then creep outside and ring the door bell.

You: What happened to the cat who swallowed the wool?
Mom: I give up.
You: She had mittens.

Equipment: A glass and some clingfilm.
Joke: Stretch the clingfilm very tightly over your Dad's glass of wine when he's not looking and wait till he tries to drink from it.

You: Why did Dracula take medicine?
Dad: I give up.
You: To stop his coffin.

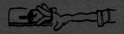

Equipment: A kitchen clock.
Joke: Get up before everyone else and change the kitchen clock to half an hour later. That'll get your brother running for school.

You: Where would you find an extinct cow?
Mom: I give up.
You: In a moo-seum.

Equipment: An empty wine bottle and some blackcurrant juice.
Joke: Fill the bottle up with the juice and put it back in the wine rack.

You: How do you stop an elephant from charging?
Dad: I give up.
You: You take away his credit cards.

Equipment: An empty whiskey
bottle and some cold tea.
Joke: Fill the bottle up with the
cold tea and put it back in the
drinks cupboard.

You: Why are elephants all wrinkly?
Mom: I give up.
You: Have you ever tried to iron
one?

Equipment: A bunch of carrots.
Joke: Stick these behind your ears
and wait for your mom to notice.

You: What did the dentist ask the
chef?
Dad: I give up.
You: Can I do the filling?

Equipment: Some boiled eggs.
Joke: Scoop out the middle and turn them upside down in the egg-cup. Then invite the rest of the family to join you for breakfast.

You: Who was the chef's favorite composer?
Mom: I give up.
You: Ludwig van Bakeoven.

Equipment: Some string.
Joke: Tie the end of the spoon with the string and then mysteriously pull it across the table when your brother tries to pick it up to eat his ice cream.

You: Which saint always had flu?
Dad: I give up.
You: Saint Francis of Asneezi.

Equipment: A living room clock.
Joke: When your Dad falls asleep on the sofa after lunch, wind the clock forwards one hour.

You: What did the mommy bee say to the baby?
Mom: I give up.
You: Beehive yourself.

Equipment: A little brother.
Joke: Send your brother to the
shop to buy you one litre of tartan
paint.

You: What did the male centipede
say about the female?
Dad: I give up.
You: She's got a nice pair of legs,
pair of legs, pair of legs...

Equipment: A CD Rack.
Joke: If your Dad alphabetizes all
his CDs go in when he's at work
and swap them all round. But
watch out when he gets back.

You: What do you do with an
excess of steel wool?
Mom: I give up.
You: Knit yourself a car.

Equipment: A birthday.
Joke: Get up early and hide all your sister's birthday cards. Just when she looks really miserable, shower her with them.

You: What's the computer's favorite snack?
Dad: I give up.
You: Microchips.

Equipment: Some cotton and a piece of material.

Joke: Tie the material to the cotton and then hang it from your parents' wardrobe. After they've gone to bed start wiggling the cotton from outside the room and they'll think they've got a ghost.

You: What's the cannibal's favorite dinner?

Mom: I give up.

You: Fish and chaps.

Equipment: A tape recorder.
Joke: Make a recording of the telephone ringing and then play it every time your Dad gets into the bath.

You: What did the Spanish farmer say to his hens?
Dad: I give up.
You: Oh, Lay!

Equipment: One small stone and a piece of string.

Joke: Tie string around stone and suspend on outside of window frame (better if it's breezy). When your Dad goes out to investigate the tapping at the window, nab his seat by the TV.

You: What bird is always breathless?

Mom: I give up.

You: A puffin.

Equipment: A pair of pajamas.
Joke: Get ready for school and then put your pajamas over the top; get back into bed and pretend to be late. Your mom will be really embarrassed after she starts telling you off.

You: What wobbles as it flies?
Dad: I give up.
You: A jellycopter.

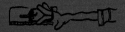

Equipment: Every alarm clock in the house.

Joke: Wait till your teenage sister has had a late night out with her friends and then leave all the alarm clocks next to her bed to go off very early the next morning.

You: Why did the dog go to court?
Dad: I give up.
You: Because it got a barking ticket.

Equipment: A hole punch.
Joke: Punch a large hole in the plastic sugar spoon and then wait for your aunty to try and put some sugar in her tea.

You: Why did the faucet run?
Mom: I give up.
You: Because it saw the kitchen sink.

Equipment: A tape with spooky noises.

Joke: Pre-record a tape with spooky noises and when you go on holiday, tell your family you heard from the locals that the house is haunted. Then switch the tape on during the night.

You: What did the mommy vampire say to her daughter?
Mom: I give up.
You: Drink your soup before it clots.

Equipment: Some postcards of chimpanzees.
Joke: Cut out the faces and stick them over you and your family's own faces on cherished group photos.

You: What did the daddy ghost say to his son?
Dad: I give up.
You: Spook when you're spooken to.

Equipment: A little brother.
Joke: Teach your sibling to speak backwards and then be rude about your parents without their knowing.

You: Where does Cruella de Ville keep her money?
Mom: I give up.
You: In a blood bank.

Equipment: Some old newspaper.
Joke: Stuff the newspaper down
the bottom of your sister's
Wellington boots and wait till it
rains and she tries to put them on.

You: What do you call a contented,
friendly monster?
Dad: I give up.
You: A failure.

Equipment: A lot of old envelopes that look new.
Joke: Reseal them all secretly and then creep down early in the morning so that your parents think they have a huge wad of fan mail.

You: What athlete is warmest in winter?
Mom: I give up.
You: The long jumper.

Equipment: A tape recorder.
Joke: Record the theme tune of
your father's favorite TV program
and then start playing it as soon as
he goes to make a cup of coffee.
He'll run back in thinking that he's
missed the beginning.

You: What does King Arthur say
when he goes to bed?
Dad: I give up.
You: Good Knight.

Equipment: Some tiny bells.
Joke: Buy some of these in a pet shop and then tie them underneath your parents' bed.

You: What does the soldier say when you buy him a drink?
Mom: I give up.
You: Tank you.

Equipment: Some cold jacket
potatoes.
Joke: Gather the uneaten potatoes
and put them underneath the
bottom sheet in your sister's bed.
Wait to see how she squelches.

You: What was Noah's mission in
life?
Dad: I give up.
You: Preserving pears.

Equipment: An out-of-date key.
Joke: Wait till your parents are
watching and then say "whoops"
and drop the key down the drain.

You: What's yellow and stays hot in
the fridge?
Mom: I give up.
You: Mustard.

Equipment: A shampoo bottle.
Joke: Wait till your father is about to wash his hair then crack an egg into the shampoo bottle. As soon as he runs hot water on his hair the egg will start to scramble.

You: Where did the newly-wed rabbits go?
Dad: I give up.
You: On bunnymoon.

Equipment: A clean sheet.
Joke: Fold your sibling's sheet in half so that both ends are at the pillow end of the bed. Replace the top cover and watch them trying to get in.

You: Why did the teacher write on her toes?
Mom: I give up.
You: She was adding a footnote.

Equipment: Some shoelaces.
Joke: When your Dad falls asleep
on the sofa, tie his shoelaces
together.

You: What do you give an injured
lemon?
Dad: I give up.
You: Lemon-aid.

Equipment: A sibling.
Joke: Pretend to argue with your brother and every time you "hit" each other, make loud noises by slapping your hands together. This can look very realistic.

You: What did one pencil say to the other?
Mom: I give up.
You: I've got a leadache.

Equipment: Tomato ketchup.
Joke: Pour some tomato ketchup
on your sleeve and then shout out
for help from your terrified mother
(but do tell her immediately that
it's fake).

You: Why can't a leopard hide?
Dad: I give up.
You: Because it will always be
spotted.

Equipment: A pair of pajamas and some other clothes.

Joke: Put the pajamas into your bed and stuff them with other clothes. Then hide under the bed and wait for your parents to come and bid you good night.

You: Why did the tightrope walker visit the bank?

Mom: I give up.

You: To check his balance.

Equipment: A bar of soap.
Joke: Use a bar of soap to "draw" a crack on the bathroom mirror. This is very realistic so explain the joke to your parents fairly rapidly.

You: How do you mend a pogo stick?
Dad: I give up.
You: Give it a spring clean.

Equipment: Sticky black paper.
Joke: Just before a big family
photo occasion, stick pieces of
black paper over your teeth and
then grin broadly into the camera.

You: Why is a pig like ink?
Mom: I give up.
You: They both belong in a pen.

Equipment: Thumbnails.
Joke: Tell your parents that you think you have broken your nose. Put your hands on either side of your nose while secretly clicking your thumbnails against your teeth.

You: Who was purple and conquered the world?
Dad: I give up.
You: Alexander the Grape.

Equipment: A piece of card and some string.

Joke: When your Dad falls asleep in front of the television, write "Science Museum – Exhibit 245" on the card and hang it around his neck.

You: Why did the cookie go to the doctor?

Mom: I give up.

You: Because it felt crummy.

Equipment: A piece of card and some string.

Joke: When your sister falls asleep in front of the television, write "Sleeping Beauty" on the card and hang it around her neck.

You: What do you say when the skeleton goes abroad?

Dad: I give up.

You: Bone voyage.

Equipment: Sugar and salt.
Joke: Swap the contents of the salt mill and the sugar pot around but make sure you run for it before your dad starts drinking his coffee.

You: What's the best day for cooking bacon?
Mom: I give up.
You: Fryday.

At School

Equipment: Several friends and an English lesson.

Joke: Ask several friends how to spell "Monopoly" then start shouting out "NO-NO" as soon as they answer. When they give up just say you were trying to help by giving them the third and fourth letters.

You: What's the snake's favorite lesson?

Teacher: I give up.

You: Hisss-tory.

Equipment: A straw and a pin.
Joke: Prick two tiny holes at either end of the straw and then lend it to a friend at lunch. No matter how hard they suck, it will not work.

You: In which battle was Lord Nelson killed?
Teacher: I give up.
You: His last one.

Equipment: A science lesson.
Joke: Say to your friend that frozen water is iced water and then ask them that if this is so, then what's frozen ink? They will answer "I stink."

You: Who designed King Arthur's Round Table?
Teacher: I give up.
You: Sir Cumference.

Equipment: A piece of paper.
Joke: Write the word "What" on a piece of paper and fold it up. Tell your friend you know what they're going to say next. They're bound to say "What?"

You: Which Scottish leader was very thin?
Teacher: I give up.
You: Boney Prince Charlie.

Equipment: Several friends and a math lesson.

Joke: Tell several friends that a train left Norwich with seven passengers and then say how many passengers got on and off at the next five stations. Then ask how many times the train stopped.

You: Why did Napoleon wear his hat sideways?

Teacher: I give up.

You: So the enemy wouldn't know which way he was going.

Equipment: A class full of pupils.
Joke: Start yawning loudly and visibly in a lesson and soon everyone else will be yawning too.

You: Why was Henry V like a book?
Teacher: I give up.
You: Because he had loads of pages.

Equipment: A lunch break.
Joke: Ask your friend where your cream cake has disappeared to. They say they don't know and you suggest a counting game. You say "I one it." They say "I two it" and so on. When they get to "I eight it," say "I knew it all along."

You: What instrument did the ancient Britons play?
Teacher: I give up.
You: The Anglo-Saxophone.

Equipment: A gym lesson.
Joke: Tell the teacher you can jump higher than a house. When they say that you can't, tell them that a house can't jump.

You: How did Chief Sitting Bull send secret messages?
Teacher: I give up.
You: He used smokeless fuel.

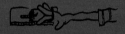

Equipment: A friend.
Joke: Ask your friend if they had the television on last night and when they say " yes" ask them how it fit.

You: How did Christopher Columbus save money?
Teacher: I give up.
You: He went across the Atlantic on one galleon.

Equipment: Two carrots and a science lesson.

Joke: Cut up the carrot and put it in the fish tank. When the teacher comes along, pull out the carrot, stick it in your mouth and say "yum, yum."

You: What do pixies do after school?

Teacher: I give up.

You: Gnomework.

Equipment: Several friends and an English lesson.

Joke: Tell several pupils that "Serendipity" is a long word and ask them to spell it. When they give up, say "I-T."

You: How do you define the word "explain"?

Teacher: I give up.

You: Eggs without mayonnaise.

Equipment: A coin.
Joke: Tell your friend you're going to place the coin where everyone in the room can see it except her. Then put it on her head.

You: How do you define the phrase "ghost writer?"
Teacher: I give up.
You: A spooksman.

Equipment: One stiff piece of card.

Joke: Attend a gymnastics class and when one of the other pupils does the splits tear the card briskly, making a loud ripping sound.

You: Why did the schoolboy hate decimals?

Teacher: I give up.

You: He couldn't see the point.

Equipment: A nail bent in the middle by a parent.

Joke: Wear the nail around your finger in class so that it looks as if it goes right through you. Then lift your finger up and start howling.

You: What do rabbits want to be when they leave school?

Teacher: I give up.

You: Million-hares.

Equipment: A math class.
Joke: Ask your friends to write down the number eleven thousand, eleven hundred and eleven. Most of them will write the number 11,1111 when the total sum of all three numbers in fact comes to 12,111.

You: Why did the cyclops close his school?
Teacher: I give up.
You: Because he only had one pupil.

Equipment: An English lesson.
Joke: Tell your friends that there are only eleven letters in the alphabet. Then count the letters in the words "the alphabet."

You: How did Nobel invent gunpowder?
Teacher: I give up.
You: It came to him in a flash.

Equipment: A lump of cheese.
Joke: Put a lump of cheese inside an unused school locker and then wait a few days. No one will be able to work out what the awful stink is or where it's coming from.

You: Who was the first podiatrist?
Teacher: I give up.
You: William the Corncurer.

Equipment: A green pot scourer.
Joke: Plant this in a small garden pot with some earth and tell your science teacher that it's a rare cactus.

You: What were the Tsar's children called?
Teacher: I give up.
You: Tsardines.

Equipment: A math lesson and some gray eyeshadow.
Joke: Pretend to fall off your chair in the math lesson and secretly smudge around your eye with the eyeshadow. You're bound to get the afternoon off.

You: Why is history the sweetest lesson?
Teacher: I give up.
You: Because it's full of dates.

Equipment: Two pieces of paper and a rubber band.

Joke: Roll each piece of paper into a tube and twist it in the middle. Put both twists through the rubber band, winding them round as you go. Place this under someone's exercise book and it will spin wildly the next time they pick it up.

You: Where do you find the Andes?

Teacher: I give up.

You: At the end of the wristies.

Equipment: Two sausages.
Joke: In your biology lesson, put two sausages in the plant tray and tell your teacher that there are monster worms in the lettuce.

You: What does the teacher have that the pupils don't?
Teacher: I give up.
You: The answer book.

Equipment: A pencil and paper.
Joke: Bet your friend in the library that they can't write a small letter "i" with a dot over it. When they write a regular letter "i," tell them they've forgotten the extra dot over the top.

You: What two plays did Shakespeare write at lunchtime?
Teacher: I give up.
You: Hamlet and Offalo.

In the Playground

Equipment: Several friends and a lunch break.

Joke: Tell your friends you know an ancient magic chant and they should sit down and repeat "O WHA-TANINNY-IAM." They will soon end up saying "Oh what a ninny I am."

You: My mom's gone to the Caribbean.

Schoolmate: Jamaica?

You: No, she wanted to go.

Equipment: A daft friend.
Joke: Bet your friend you can make them say the word "tomato." Ask them what their favorite juice is and when they say "apple" say "I win." When they protest that you only mentioned tomato, then you can say "Now I really win."

You: What paper do cats read?
Schoolmate: I give up.
You: The Daily Mews.

Equipment: A cup of water.
Joke: Bet your friends that you can knock the cup on the floor without spilling any of the water. Then kneel down and tap the cup on the floor.

You: What do you give an injured parrot?
Schoolmate: I give up.
You: Tweetment.

Equipment: A coin.
Joke: Tell your friend to take a coin out of his pocket and then say you can tell the date. When he looks disbelieving, tell him today's date.

You: Which Muppet is hard to see through?
Schoolmate: I give up.
You: Kermit the Fog.

Equipment: Some mascara.
Joke: Tell your friend she has
some dirt on her nose and when
she asks you to wipe it off,
completely cover the tip of her
nose with the mascara.

You: How does King Kong
overcome obstacles?
Schoolmate: I give up.
You: He puts his beast foot
forward.

Equipment: A handkerchief and a squash ball.

Joke: Sew the squash ball into the centre of the hanky and then, after you're blown your nose with it, throw it on the floor.

You: What do you get if you cross a cow with an Arab leader?

Schoolmate: I give up.

You: A milk sheik.

Equipment: A playground.
Joke: Bet your friend that you can jump across the playground. Walk over to the other side of the playground and then jump.

You: What do you get if you cross a lamb with a radiator?
Schoolmate: I give up.
You: Central bleating.

Equipment: A line-up of friends.
Joke: Bet all your friends that they can't copy you exactly. Line them up and bend down on one knee. Lift one arm in the air. Gently give a shove to the left and, with a bit of luck, they will all topple over like dominoes.

You: What did the bald man say when he got a comb for a present?
Schoolmate: I give up.
You: It's fantastic! I'll never part with it.

Equipment: Two plastic spoons and some honey.

Joke: Get two friends to kneel opposite each other and try to tap each other on the head with plastic spoons. After a while, secretly put some honey in one of the spoons and then watch it trickle.

You: What did the judge say when a skunk ran into court?

Schoolmate: I give up.

You: Odor in the court.

Equipment: Some newspaper and a pair of gloves.
Joke: Stuff your gloves with the paper and attach them to the ends of your sleeves with elastic. Then offer to shake hands with your friends.

You: How come the monsters got engaged?
Schoolmate: I give up.
You: It was love at first fright.

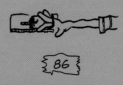

Equipment: A photocopier and a ten dollar bill.
Joke: Photocopy a ten dollar bill ten times and then watch your friends' faces as you tear up the fake bills in the playground.

You: Which monster gorilla really stinks?
Schoolmate: I give up.
You: King Pong.

Equipment: Two cups of water.
Joke: Fill two paper cups with water and then put them on the backs of your friend's hands and tell him to remove them without spilling any liquid. When they give up, tell them to drink the water from one of the cups.

You: What do astronauts have for their tea?
Schoolmate: I give up.
You: Launcheon meat.

Equipment: Three chairs.
Joke: Line three chairs up and then say that you will take your shoes off before you jump over them. Take your shoes off and jump over your shoes.

You: What did they call the boy who was named after his father?
Schoolmate: I give up.
You: Dad.

Equipment: A book.
Joke: Bet your friend that they can kiss the book on the inside and the outside without even opening it. Kiss it once on the cover, then run inside and kiss it again.

You: What did they say about the banker who got bored with his job?
Schoolmate: I give up.
You: He lost interest.

Equipment: Two hands.
Joke: Stand facing the corner of the playground with your arms crossed and both hands just peeking out around your back or neck and squirming around. It will look as though you are cuddling someone.

You: Why did the boy shoot the clock?
Schoolmate: I give up.
You: He was trying to kill time.

Equipment: A group of friends.
Joke: Tell them that the Queen is coming to your school next week to unveil a swingcost. When they ask you "what's a swingcost?", tell them "about $100."

You: How do you swim a hundred meters in two seconds?
Schoolmate: I give up.
You: Swim over a waterfall.

Equipment: A piece of wood.
Joke: Tell your friend you can lift him or her to the top of the bike shed. Blindfold the friend and then lift him so he can touch the piece of wood you are holding just above his head.

You: Where does a ten-tonne elephant sleep?
Schoolmate: I give up.
You: Anywhere it wants to.

Equipment: A pencil.

Joke: Hold a pencil in your left hand and tap it three times on the floor, betting your friends that they can't do the same. Nine times out of ten your friends will use their right hand and therefore get it wrong.

You: What did the oil and vinegar say to the fridge?

Schoolmate: I give up.

You: Shut the door, we're dressing.

Equipment: A paper bag.
Joke: Hold the paper bag open and then pretend to catch things in it. After several flicks, show your friends an empty bag. (This one needs practice.)

You: Why do cows wear bells?
Schoolmate: I give up.
You: Because their horns don't work.

Equipment: A hat and a glass of water.

Joke: Cover the glass with the hat. Bet your friends that you can drink the water without touching the hat. Bend down, make a slurping noise and say you've finished. The friends will then remove the hat to check it's true, at which point you grab the glass and drink the water without having touched the hat.

You: What did one historian say to the other?
Schoolmate: I give up.
You: Let's talk about old times.

You: What do gorillas learn at school?
Schoolmate: I give up.
You: Their Ape-B-C.

Equipment: A daft friend.
Joke: Ask you friend what subject
snakes are best at. When they give
up, say "sss-cience."

You: What's Dracula's favorite
sport?
Schoolmate: I give up.
You: Bat-minton.

Equipment: A glass of water.
Joke: Bet your friends that you can sing under water. When they don't believe you, start singing while pouring the water onto your head.

You: What does a bird use for an emergency landing?
Schoolmate: I give up.
You: His sparrowchute.

Equipment: A hard-boiled egg.
Joke: Tell your friends you can
jump on an egg without breaking
it. Get your previously hard-boiled
egg from your pocket and lay it
down. Jump but just touch the egg
with your feet. With practice it
won't even crack.

You: Which creatures didn't go into
Noah's ark in pairs?
Schoolmate: I give up.
You: Maggots – they went in
apples.

Equipment: A silly friend.
Joke: Tell your friend that you're not going to grow bananas any longer. When she asks why not, say it's because they're long enough already.

You: Which fish is musical?
Schoolmate: I give up.
You: A piano tuna.

Equipment: An empty matchbox.
Joke: Cut the end out of the inside tray and stick your finger through secretly. When you open the matchbox to show your friends it will look as if there's a severed finger inside.

You: Where do sheep get their hair cut?
Schoolmate: I give up.
You: At the baa-baa's shop.

Equipment: A schoolmate.

Joke: Ask your schoolmate what they would do, if they came across a bear in the forest coming straight towards them and when they say "run for it," reply "with a bear behind?"

You: What's an Australian's favorite drink?

Schoolmate: I give up.

You: Coca-Koala.

Friends

Equipment: A large book, a packet of flour and a scarf.
Joke: Tell your friend that he must kneel down blindfold and kiss the magic book. When he does, swap the book for a packet of flour.

You: What do you call a naked pig?
Friend: I give up.
You: Streaky bacon.

Equipment: A friend.
Joke: Tell your friend that you can turn them into a Red Indian and when they say "how?", say "you see, it works."

You: How do frogs send messages?
Friend: I give up.
You: Morse Toad.

Equipment: A sheet, a flashlight and a wet sponge.

Joke: Tell your friend that you're going to show her a tropical storm in the jungle. Get two friends to hold up the sheet while a third friend switches the flashlight on and off through it. As your friend gets up, splosh the wet sponge in her face.

You: What's a Grecian urn?
Friend: I give up.
You: $50 per week.

Equipment: A paper cup and a pin.
Joke: Use the pin to make a few
small holes just below the rim of
the cup so your friend can't see
them. Then fill it up with
something delicious and watch
your friend trying to work out why
it leaks all over his sleeve.

You: What do naughty eggs do?
Friend: I give up.
You: Play practical yolks.

Equipment: A raw sausage.
Joke: Put a sausage between two of your fingers. Shake your friend's hand and say "ouch" then pull your hand away leaving them holding the sausage.

You: What does a disciplined librarian have?
Friend: I give up.
You: Shelf-control.

Equipment: Two hairbrushes.
Joke: Put these down the bottom
of your friend's bed with the
spokes facing toward the pillow.
When your friend gets into bed,
he'll think there's a hedgehog
down there.

You: Who makes clothes out of
spinach?
Friend: I give up.
You: Popeye the tailor man.

Equipment: A daft friend.
Joke: Bet your friend they can't answer four questions wrongly. Ask three easy questions and then say "that's three I've asked now, isn't it?" They will immediately reply "yes" and you've won the bet.

You: Why did the bald man go outside?
Friend: I give up.
You: To get some fresh hair.

Equipment: A friend with a hand.
Joke: Take your friend's hand and say "Good morning I'm the milkman" then wring their hand and make a mooing noise.

You: What's green and booming?
Friend: I give up.
You: A froghorn.

Equipment: A sweater.
Joke: Pretend something from behind you has grabbed you around the neck then roll your sleeve up on one arm and pretend to strangle yourself.

You: What do you call a cow who eats grass?
Friend: I give up.
You: A lawn moo-er.

Equipment: Another friend with a hand.

Joke: Take your friend's hand and say "Good morning I'm the electricity man" then press your finger into their palm and make a buzzing noise.

You: Why did the coffee taste like mud?

Friend: I give up.

You: Because it was ground this morning.

Equipment: A third friend with a hand.

Joke: Take your friend's hand and say "Good morning I'm the carpenter" then press your finger into their palm and make drilling noises.

You: When do ghosts play tricks?
Friend: I give up.
You: On April Ghoul's Day.

Equipment: A hand with some fingers.

Joke: Hold your hand out with your palm and fingers facing upwards then ask your friend to guess what it is. When they give up turn your hand over and say "A dead one of these."

You: Who's always up on current affairs?

Friend: I give up.

You: The electrician.

Equipment: Two fingers and a thumb.

Joke: Hold your hand with two fingers and a thumb pointing upwards. Explain to your puzzled friend that this is Sooty with no clothes on.

You: Why do they call money "dough?"

Friend: I give up.

You: Because everybody kneads it.

Equipment: A loud voice.
Joke: As your friend cycles by, point to their back wheel and shout out "your back wheel's going around." Strangely, they will almost always get off to have a look.

You: Why did the potatoes argue?
Friend: I give up.
You: They couldn't see eye to eye.

Equipment: Ten fingers.

Joke: Tell your friend you have eleven fingers. Count them one to ten and then go backwards from ten to six and point out that the other hand has another five – making a grand total of eleven.

You: Why did the man put his wife under the bed at night?

Friend: I give up.

You: Because she's a little potty.

Equipment: A friend, a sheet and a sleepover.

Joke: Get one of your friends to pretend they've already gone to bed and then start reading the others a ghost story. At a suitably spooky moment, get your friend to re-enter the room in a sheet.

You: Why did the boy go to night school?

Friend: I give up.

You: Because he wanted to learn to read in the dark.

Equipment: A pair of sandals and a sweater.

Joke: Put the sandals on the table with your hands in them and wear your sweater back to front. Stamp your hands up and down in your shoes and your friend will think you're an angry baby.

You: How do you hire a horse?
Friend: I give up.
You: Put a brick under each hoof.

Equipment: Two thumbs.
Joke: Bend your thumbs together in the middle and then hide the join with a finger. Call out that you have cut your thumb off and then move your thumbs apart.

You: What do you call a fish with no eyes?
Friend: I give up.
You: A fsh.

Equipment: A walnut.

Joke: Tell your friend that they're about to see something that's never been seen before and will never be seen again. Crack the shell to reveal the walnut and then eat it.

You: Where do you find giant snails?

Friend: I give up.

You: At the end of giant's fingers.

Equipment: A piece of paper.
Joke: Make a very small pinprick in the center of the paper and then ask your friends if they can push their finger through the center of the paper without tearing it. After they give up, roll the paper into a tube and stick your finger through the center.

You: Where do cows go on Saturday nights?
Friend: I give up.
You: To the moovies.

Equipment: A pen and paper.
Joke: Say to your friend: "I can write with my left ear." When they refuse to believe you take the pen and write the words "with my left ear."

You: Where do cows go for a good night out?
Friend: I give up.
You: To a moosical.

Equipment: Another pen and paper.

Joke: Say to your friend "I can push myself through a keyhole." When they don't believe you, write "myself" on a piece of paper and stuff it through a keyhole.

Neighbors

Equipment: Two buckets and a snowstorm.

Joke: After it snows, go out into your neighbor's garden wearing buckets on either feet and then add small toe marks to the huge Yeti footprints you have already created.

You: What does a swimmer wear to work?

Neighbor: I give up.

You: A swimsuit.

Equipment: Some newspaper and a jacket potato.

Joke: Wrap the potato up in twenty-five layers of newspaper and then offer it to your neighbor for her birthday.

You: Why did the ants play football in the saucer?

Neighbor: I give up.

You: They were practicing for the cup.

Equipment: A piece of cotton and a small stick.

Joke: Tie the cotton to your neighbor's window and hang the stick onto the cotton. Next time there's a storm, it will sound just like a ghost.

You: Why is skiing becoming less popular?

Neighbor: I give up.

You: Because it's rapidly going downhill.

Equipment: A bunch of bananas.
Joke: When your neighbor is out,
gently stick a needle through the
skin of each banana and then
wiggle it up and down. When the
bananas are peeled, it will seem as
if they are already sliced.

You: What flavour jam do
cheerleaders like?
Neighbor: I give up.
You: Rah-rah-rahspberry.

Equipment: A packet of liver salts.
Joke: Fill your neighbor's sugar pot
with liver salts and watch their tea
fizz!

You: What monkey flies fast?
Neighbor: I give up.
You: King Kongcorde.

Equipment: A silly neighbor.
Joke: Warn your neighbor that there's a dogweigh on his back. When he asks you "what's a dogweigh?" reply "five kilos."

You: Why don't you tell pigs secrets?
Neighbor: I give up.
You: Because they squeal.

Equipment: Some raspberry jam.
Joke: Next time your neighbor's
Dad bends over to shake your
hand make sure you have some
raspberry jam in your palm.

You: What can you serve but never
eat?
Neighbor: I give up.
You: A tennis ball.

Equipment: A good pair of lungs.
Joke: Open your mouth wide and suck in some air while simultaneously growling. Do this again very rapidly and you will sound like a parrot in the Amazon jungle, really confusing your neighbors.

You: What is Dracula's favorite fruit?
Neighbor: I give up.
You: Neck-tarines.

Equipment: A $5 bill and some thread.

Joke: Stick the thread to the $5 bill and then leave it to lie in the garden while you hold onto the thread through the fence. When your neighbor tries to pick it up, whip the note away using the thread.

You: Who invented the plane that didn't fly?

Neighbor: I give up.

You: The Wrong Brothers.

Equipment: Some broken china.
Joke: Save the pieces of broken china and wrap them up beautifully in a box. Go round to your neighbor's with a "special surprise gift" and then pretend to slip over just as you are presenting your generous offering.

You: What do toads eat with their hamburgers?
Neighbor: I give up.
You: French flies.

Equipment: One shiny coin and a tube of superglue.
Joke: Glue the coin to your neighbors' drive and watch them cursing as they try to pick it up.

You: What's the frog's favorite ballet?
Neighbor: I give up.
You: Swamp Lake.

Equipment: A potato.

Joke: Peel a potato and then cut it into the same shape as your thumb. Hold the potato in place on your hand instead of your thumb and then stick pins in it.

You: Why does the pig buy bacon?
Neighbor: I give up.
You: To get his own back.

Equipment: A white sheet.

Joke: Choose a window that your neighbors can see into and then dress up in the white sheet when they aren't expecting it and make scary noises.

You: What did the golf ball say to the club?

Neighbor: I give up.

You: Come up and tee me some time.

Equipment: A flashlight.
Joke: Stand outside your neighbor's kitchen window at night and shine the flashlight up at your face while maintaining a scary expression.

You: What do top cats strive to achieve?
Neighbor: I give up.
You: Purrr-fection.

Equipment: A mailbox.
Joke: Wait until your neighbor is watching and then pretend to mail a letter and get your hand stuck. Wait patiently while they try to help you.

You: What do you call a silly ape?
Neighbor: I give up.
You: A chump-anzee.

Equipment: A mailbox.
Joke: Wait until your neighbor passes by and then start talking to the mailbox, pretending that your friend is stuck inside.

You: What do you call a flea on the moon?
Neighbor: I give up.
You: A lunar-tick.

Equipment: A pot of cherry stones.
Joke: Hide up a tree and drop these on your neighbor's head when he comes out into the garden.

You: How do you chop up the sea?
Neighbor: I give up.
You: With a sea-saw.

Equipment: A healthy pair of arms.
Joke: Go into your garden and point vigorously at your neighbor's garden. They'll spend hours looking for the fault.

You: Why is my dog called Camera?
Neighbor: I give up.
You: Because he's always snapping.

Equipment: A tree.

Joke: Stand behind your tree and put your palms and thumbs together, clasping your fingers around your fists. Blow between the knuckles of your thumbs and your neighbors will think they have an owl in the garden.

You: What did the woodpecker say to the tree?

Neighbor: I give up.

You: It's been nice gnawing you.

Equipment: A broken cup and some plasticine.
Joke: Stick the handle back on the cup with the plasticine and then offer your neighbor a nice cup of tea.

You: Why was Cinderella banned from soccer practice?
Neighbor: I give up.
You: Because she kept running away from the ball.

Equipment: A spool of cotton.
Joke: Hide a spool of cotton up your sweater and then let a little piece hang loose on the outside. Your neighbor will helpfully try and pull it off only to discover the piece getting longer and longer.

You: What sandals do frogs wear?
Neighbor: I give up.
You: Open-toad.

Equipment: Some string.
Joke: Tie the handles of two of your neighbor's bedrooms together with a piece of string while there are people inside both of them. When one opens a door, the other will mysteriously close.

You: What game is played by twenty people in a lift?
Neighbor: I give up.
You: Squash.

Equipment: A long tape measure.
Joke: Tell one of your neighbors that you've got to measure his house for a school project. Get him to hold one end of a tape measure and then do the same thing to your neighbor on the other side.

You: Where do urban pigs live?
Neighbor: I give up.
You: In sty-scrapers.

Enemies

Equipment: An apple and some locks of hair.

Joke: Carve an apple into a head shape and stick the hair on. When it's dry, leave it on your enemy's desk and they'll get quite a shock.

You: Who's Britain's worst athlete?
Enemy: I give up.
You: The man who ran a bath and came second.

Equipment: An enemy.
Joke: Ask your enemy if they collect stamps and when they say they do, then stamp on their foot (but not too violently).

You: What did one traffic light say to the other?
Enemy: I give up.
You: Don't look, I'm changing.

Equipment: A pair of socks and some thread.

Joke: Sew up your enemy's socks at the open end. They will spend ages puzzling over this.

You: What happened to the man who fell into the beer?

Enemy: I give up.

You: He came to a bitter end.

Equipment: A lump of cheese.
Joke: Next time you are at your enemy's house and they leave the room, quickly pull the decorative end off their curtain rod and insert the lump of cheese. They'll never work out where the rotten smell is coming from.

You: What happened to the woman who fell into the toffee?
Enemy: I give up.
You: She came to a sticky end.

Equipment: Some tea.
Joke: Offer your enemy a nice cup of tea but make it with cold water.

You: What happened to the owl who was crossed with a skunk?
Enemy: I give up.
You: He stank but he didn't give a hoot.

Equipment: A box of tissues and some glue.
Joke: Take all the tissues out of the box. Stick them end to end with the glue and then replace them in the box. Leave them around when your enemy has a cold.

You: What happened to the skunk who was crossed with a salad?
Enemy: I give up.
You: She stank but she didn't give a toss.

Equipment: Some potatoes and some toffee.

Joke: On Halloween hand your enemy a potato covered in toffee and then watch them try and chew their "toffee apple."

You: Why is the theater so tragic?
Enemy: I give up.
You: Because the audience is in tiers.

Equipment: A doorway.

Joke: Tell your enemy to stand in a doorway and press the backs of her hands for one minute against the frame of the door. When the minute is up, tell her to "stick 'em up" – and she will.

You: How do ghosts travel?

Enemy: I give up.

You: United Scarelines.

Equipment: A crowded coach on a school trip.
Joke: Tell your enemy that everyone on the bus is going to shout out the word "Teletubbies" as soon as you raise your left hand. As soon as the bus is really quiet, raise your left hand.

You: Who haunts hospitals?
Enemy: I give up.
You: Surgical spirits.

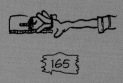

Equipment: Some peas, a yoghurt pot and a tray.

Joke: Put the peas in the pot on a tray in your enemy's bedroom. Just before he or she goes to bed, pour some hot water on the peas. They will soon expand and pop out of the pot, landing on the tray with an explosive bang.

You: What does one ghost say to the other?

Enemy: I give up.

You: Do you believe in people?

Equipment: A cloth and an enemy's watch.

Joke: Tell your enemy that you're going to show them a brilliant magic trick using their watch. Fold it inside the cloth but, secretly, sneak it out the side. Smash the cloth with a hammer and then say "whoops, the trick's gone wrong."

You: What do you call a wicked devil?
Enemy: I give up.
You: Sir.

Equipment: Some paper serviettes and a beaker.

Joke: Tell your enemy that it's a well-known fact that if you get down on your hands and knees and stick a serviette on your head while blowing hard into a beaker, then the serviette will fly up into the air.

You: Where do sheep go on vacation?

Enemy: I give up.

You: The Baa-hamas.

Equipment: A cup and a stick.
Joke: Stand on a chair and position the cup against the ceiling with the stick. Ask your enemy to hold it in place for a moment and then run away. She won't be able to move or she'll get all wet.

You: What did Mom Corn say to Baby Corn?
Enemy: I give up.
You: Where's Pop Corn?

Equipment: Some pipecleaners and black paint.
Joke: Paint the pipecleaners black and then tie them together to look like a spider. Attach this to your victim's bedroom ceiling.

You: What happened to the terrible artist?
Enemy: I give up.
You: He couldn't draw breath.

Equipment: Sticky spots.
Joke: When your enemy takes off his or her glasses, stick the spots on the outside of their glasses.

You: When do ducks get up in the morning?
Enemy: I give up.
You: At the quack of dawn.

Equipment: A coil spring and some green paint.

Joke: Paint the spring green and then put it inside your enemy's lunch box. Wait until they open it and see a snake pop out.

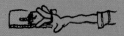

You: What does the invisible man call his mom and dad?

Enemy: I give up.

You: His trans-parents.

Equipment: A balloon and a movie ticket.

Joke: Wait till your enemy sits down at the movies then blow up a balloon without tying the neck and leave it in the seat next to him. It is bound to make an embarrassing noise.

You: Where do rabbits do national service?

Enemy: I give up.

You: In the Hare Force.

Equipment: A balloon.
Joke: Blow up a balloon and place it carefully between the door and the door frame so that it sticks. When your enemy opens the door it will whizz out and make a weird noise.

You: What do you call a man with greasy hair?
Enemy: I give up.
You: Chip.

Equipment: A packet of flour.
Joke: Place a (lightweight) packet of flour on the top rim of the door just before your enemy enters the room. He or she will get covered in white dust.

You: What do the lions say when they see the safari trucks arrive?
Enemy: I give up.
You: Meals on Wheels!

Equipment: A tube of toothpaste.
Joke: Offer your victim a lovely cream bun when, in fact, the cream is really toothpaste that you have just squeezed all over it yourself.

You: Why did Robin Hood steal from the rich?
Enemy: I give up.
You: Because the poor didn't have anything worth stealing.

Equipment: Your mom's polka dot bra.

Joke: Tie this to the back of your enemy's backpack when they're not looking and then wait for them to set off for school.

You: Why couldn't the skeleton go to the ball?

Enemy: I give up.

You: Because it had no body to go with.

Equipment: A bright yellow post-it note.
Joke: Write on it "kiss me quick" and stick it on your enemy's back.

You: Why did Humpty Dumpty get into trouble at school?
Enemy: I give up.
You: Because he cracked up in class.

Equipment: Some yellow chalk.
Joke: Write a message on your
hand in chalk and then pat your
enemy on the back so that the
message is transferred onto their
favorite dark jumper.

You: Why was the sand wet?
Enemy: I give up.
You: Because the sea weed.

Equipment: Torn up pieces of paper.

Joke: Find your enemy's umbrella and fill it with torn up pieces of paper. Next time it rains they'll get a headful of confetti.

You: How did Noah see in the dark?

Enemy: I give up.

You: He used flood lights.

Equipment: An enemy.
Joke: Tell the enemy that there were three idiots sitting on a wall – Do, Ray and Me. Do and Ray got off so which idiot was left. The enemy, of course, will reply "me."

You: What do you call two banana skins?
Enemy: I give up.
You: A pair of slippers.

Equipment: Some red hot chilli peppers.

Joke: Stick these inside your enemy's lunchtime sandwich when they're not looking.

You: What do duck builders do?

Enemy: I give up.

You: Paper over the quacks.

Equipment: A willing friend.

Joke: Get your friend to hide at the other end of the corridor then explain to your enemy that her house has developed an echo. Every time you say something your hidden friend can echo you.

You: What does Count Dracula eat in a restaurant?

Enemy: I give up.

You: The waiter.

Equipment: A gullible enemy.
Joke: Ask your enemy to go to the local shop to buy you some elbow grease.

You: Why did the man take the saddle to bed?
Enemy: I give up.
You: In case he had night mares.

Equipment: Another gullible enemy.
Joke: Tell them that this year's spaghetti harvest just failed and wait for them to repeat this to everyone else they know.

You: Which Scottish leader constantly tumbled over?
Enemy: I give up.
YOU: Robert the Bruise.

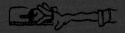

Equipment: An empty kitchen roll tube.

Joke: Paint the tube black at one end and wait an hour. Just before your enemy comes along paint the other end. Explain you've got a new telescope, holding the dry end, and then offer them the wet end to look through.

You: Who is the world's best underwater spy?

Enemy: I give up.

You: James Pond.

Equipment: A set of keys.
Joke: Swap all of the toggles round on your enemy's keys and they'll be very confused next time they try to open any doors.

You: What animal holds up your socks?
Enemy: I give up.
You: An alli-garter.

Equipment: A mirror and some ink.
Joke: Secretly mark your enemy's
pocket mirror with black ink so that
next time they sneak a look they'll
think they've suddenly got spots.

You: What do you call two parsnips
in love?
Enemy: I give up.
You: Swede-hearts.

Equipment: A hairbrush and some rice.

Joke: Secretly put the rice onto your enemy's hairbrush so that next time they brush their hair, they'll think that they've suddenly got terrible dandruff.

You: Why did the customer take his coffee black?

Enemy: I give up.

You: Because they didn't have any other colors.

Equipment: A square of red rubber.
Joke: Run up to your enemy's
kitchen window and throw the
fake brick. Explain this very quickly
or you'll be in trouble.

You: What do you call a shellfish
with a warhead attached?
Enemy: I give up.
You: A guided mussel.

Equipment: A board and some felt tip.

Joke: Make a "For Sale" sign and put it up outside your enemy's house when they've gone out.

You: What do you call a single, female spider?

Enemy: I give up.

You: A spin-ster.

Equipment: A stapler.
Joke: Staple all your enemy's papers together when they're not looking.

You: What do you call a gang of single, male spiders?
Enemy: I give up.
You: Batch-elors.

Equipment: A bottle of Tippex.
Joke: Empty the bottle out and fill
it up with milk. Leave it on your
enemy's desk.

You: Why did the dinosaur cross
the road?
Enemy: I give up.
You: Because chickens didn't exist
then.

Equipment: A telephone with labels for the numbers.
Joke: Switch round all the labels for the pre-recorded numbers and wait for confusion to ensue.

You: Where did the tenor go to jail?
Enemy: I give up.
You: Sing Sing.

Equipment: Some tape and a telephone.

Joke: Tape down the hook buttons on the telephone and when your enemy picks it up it will just carry on ringing and ringing.

You: Where do the slimey men run races?

Enemy: I give up.

You: At the Oily-impics.

Equipment: A telephone.
Joke: Phone your enemy and, imitating your teacher's voice, tell her that everyone has to wear yellow socks to school the next day.

You: Where do bald men like to live?
Enemy: I give up.
You: ManWithHatOn.

Equipment: A white sponge.
Joke: Cut this up into cubes and leave them in the sugar bowl. Wait for your enemy to try and dissolve them in a cup of tea.

You: What's the difference between a wild boar and the school bully?
Enemy: I give up.
You: One's a big, smelly stinker and the other's an animal.

Equipment: Cereal packets.
Joke: Pull the contents bags out of the cereal boxes and swap them all around. Then wait for your enemy not to pour out his favorite cereal.

You: Why are thugs like bananas?
Enemy: I give up.
You: Because they're yellow and they hang around in bunches.

Equipment: A magnet.
Joke: Stand behind your enemy with a powerful magnet when she's just had all her hair pinned up for a special evening out.

You: What do you get if you cross an idiot with a watch?
Enemy: I give up.
You: A thick tock.

Equipment: A magnet.
Joke: Stand behind your enemy
with a powerful magnet when he's
just stuffed all his favorite model
cars into his back pocket.

You: What did Santa Claus do to
the naughty reindeer?
Enemy: I give up.
You: He gave him the sack.

Equipment: Some dried grass and an empty tea packet.
Joke: Fill the empty tea packet with dried grass and wait for your victim to drink a nice cup of tea.

You: What do you call a garbage collector in a rocket?
Enemy: I give up.
You: A waste-man of space.

Equipment: Some food dye.
Joke: Secretly pour some food dye into your enemy's Smartie packet so that they all look the same and then wait for him to look for his favorite color.

You: Why did the actor fall through the floor?
Enemy: I give up.
You: It was just a stage he was going through.

Equipment: Sticky-back plastic.
Joke: Cover all your enemy's exercise books with the same color sticky-back plastic and wait for confusion to ensue.

You: Why did the patient think he was a rubber band?
Enemy: I give up.
You: Because he kept snapping at people.

Equipment: A clock.
Joke: When the teacher enemy
isn't looking, take the front off the
classroom clock and then fix
Mickey Mouse stickers to the
ends of each hand.

You: Why are bullies like toenails?
Enemy: I give up.
You: Because the sooner they're
cut down to size the better.

Equipment: A collection of computer games.
Joke: Swap all the games around inside the boxes so your enemy gets really fed up looking for his favorite.

You: What do you say to a thieving kangaroo?
Enemy: I give up.
You: Hop it.

Equipment: Some paper and a pen.
Joke: Wait till your victim leaves her house and then run up to her door and stick up a sign that says "gnome sweet gnome."

You: Why did the school pest throw away this compass?
Enemy: I give up.
You: Because everyone kept telling him to get lost.

Equipment: Some sand.
Joke: While your enemy is in his
gym class, fill up his socks with
sand and wait for his toes to start
crunching.

You: What do you get if you cross
the local bully with a yellow
pudding?
Enemy: I give up.
You: Cowardy custard.

Equipment: A felt tip pen.
Joke: When in your enemy's bedroom, secretly draw moustaches onto the posters of his or her favorite pop star. But make sure you use washable ink.

You: What do you get if you cross tapioca with an owl?
Enemy: I give up.
You: Something no one likes but it doesn't give a hoot.

Equipment: A packet of string.
Joke: Secretly add some string to
the pot when your victim tries to
cook some noodles.

You: Why did the teacher punish
the pupils for throwing jelly and
sponge around the canteen?
Enemy: I give up.
You: Because he didn't like being
trifled with.

Equipment: Sugar and salt.
Joke: Swap around the contents of the sugar and salt pots just before your enemy tries to eat his breakfast.

You: Why did the teacher tell the boy off for shouting "cock a doodle doo"?
Enemy: I give up.
You: Because he'd warned him before about using fowl language.

Equipment: Curry powder.
Joke: Offer to sprinkle some
delicious cinnamon on your
enemy's toast and then apply the
curry powder instead.

You: Why is the lazy pupil like a
river every morning?
Enemy: I give up.
You: Because he doesn't want to
leave his bed.

Equipment: Some vinegar.
Joke: Fill up an empty perfume
bottle with the vinegar and offer it
to your enemy as a birthday
present.

You: What do the witches learn at
school?
Enemy: I give up.
You: Spelling.

Equipment: Green food dye.
Joke: Siphon off the lime squash
and fill the empty bottle with plain
water colored with green dye.

You: Where do you keep souvenirs
of your fights?
Enemy: I give up.
You: In your scrap book.

Equipment: Aniseed balls.
Joke: Put aniseed balls in your enemy's cat litter and wait for the dogs to start raiding the bowl.

You: What did the three-headed monster say to the boy?
Enemy: I give up.
You: I'm keeping an eye, eye, eye on you.

Equipment: Dog food.
Joke: Empty a can of dog food into your enemy's favorite pot plant and wait for the doggies to start sniffing and scratching around.

You: What's the difference between your teenage brother and a kettle?
Enemy: I give up.
You: Nothing. They both get everyone steamed up.

Equipment: A bottle of wine.
Joke: Just before your enemy wants to throw a lavish party, put all of her wine bottles into the freezer so the liquid goes solid and she can't pour out any drinks when the guests arrive.

You: Why is my enemy a natural musician?
Enemy: I give up.
You: Because his tongue is sharp and his feet are flat.

Equipment: Blackcurrant juice.
Joke: Secretly empty out your
enemy's fountain pen and then
refill it with blackcurrant juice.

YOU: Why is my enemy like an oil
well?
Enemy: I give up.
YOU: Because he's always boring.

Equipment: Clingfilm.
Joke: Just before your enemy goes
to the toilet, cover the toilet seat
with a layer of clingfilm.

You: Why would my enemy make a
great model?
Enemy: I give up.
You: Because he's always posing.

Equipment: A walking stick.
Joke: Challenge your enemy to walk in a straight line, but first they must cover their eyes, bend over and walk briskly around the stick five times.

You: What do you get if you cross my enemy with a window?
Enemy: I give up.
You: A real pane.

Equipment: Clingfilm.

Joke: Just before your enemy takes a bite of his favorite sandwich, place a layer of clingfilm in the middle. But tell him straight away.

You: What did the camel say to his enemy?

Enemy: I give up.

You: You really give me the hump.

Equipment: Clingfilm.
Joke: Just before your enemy has a shower, stick a layer of clingfilm over the shower head and wait for her to look really puzzled (and dry).

You: Why was the hopeless burglar wrapped in silver paper?
Enemy: I give up.
You: Because he'd been foiled again.

Equipment: Washable transfers.

Joke: Just before your enemy begins his weekly ironing, secretly place a transfer on the bottom of the iron.

You: Why did the council dig a hole just there?

Enemy: I give up.

You: I don't know either but I'm looking into it.

Equipment: Washable tattoos.
Joke: When your victim takes a cat nap, secretly stick a tattoo on her arm.

You: What's the difference between a guilty man and a caterpillar?
Enemy: I give up.
You: A guilty man doesn't have a leg to stand on.

Equipment: A piece of black rubber.

Joke: Place this on the sidewalk just before your enemy walks by and wait for him to walk carefully around the huge, non-existent pothole.

You: What do you call two pip-squeaks in a shoe shop?

Enemy: I give up.

You: A pair of sneakers.

Equipment: A piece of blue rubber.
Joke: Place this on the sidewalk
just before your enemy walks by
and wait for her to walk carefully
around the huge non-existent
puddle.

You: What happened to the rude
fish?
Enemy: I give up.
YOU: He was put in his plaice.

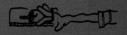

Equipment: An apple.
Joke: When it's your turn to bowl to the enemy in cricket, replace the cricket ball with a huge, ripe, red apple.

You: Why did the silly boy cut off the legs off his bed?
Enemy: I give up.
You: He wanted to lie low for a while.

Equipment: A pencil.
Joke: Just before your enemy walks down the street, draw dark lines all over the sidewalk so that she walks really carefully just to avoid the cracks.

You: Why did the idiot eat the glue?
Enemy: I give up.
You: Because he heard that school was breaking up.

Equipment: A hard-boiled egg.
Joke: Just before your enemy's crucial table tennis match, replace the ping pong ball with a carefully carved, hard-boiled egg.

You: Why did the boy wear rubber soles to the disco?
Enemy: I give up.
You: Because he wanted a job as a bouncer.

Equipment: A pot of pepper.
Joke: Shake the pepper into the bottom of your enemy's socks then watch him start scratching.

You: Which vegetable plays pool?
Enemy: I give up.
You: A cue-cumber.

Equipment: A cauliflower and some green dye.
Joke: Dye your victim's cauliflower with green dye and wait for her to prepare her favorite broccoli dinner.

You: Why is my enemy like a taxi?
Enemy: I give up.
You: Because he drives everyone away.

Equipment: A piece of coconut.
Joke: Secretly replace your victim's bar of soap with a piece of coconut white.

You: What do clever ants do when they pass an exam?
Enemy: I give up.
You: They go home and tell their par-ants.

Equipment: Some cream and a tube of toothpaste.
Joke: Secretly replace the contents of your enemy's toothpaste tube with whipping cream.

You: What's nasty and stinks and is found in my enemy's knickers?
Enemy: I give up.
You: My enemy.

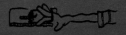

Equipment: Lemon squash.
Joke: Secretly replace the contents
of your victim's shampoo bottle
with lemon squash.

You: What did Tutankhamun do
when he got bullied?
Enemy: I give up.
You: He asked his mummy to talk
to the principal.

Equipment: A torn-up shirt.
Joke: Secretly stick a torn-up shirt in the washing machine just after your enemy takes out his washing and wait to see him think his top items are all mashed up.

You: What did the mirror say to the naughty boy?
Enemy: I give up.
You: Just watch yourself.

Equipment: A metal spring.
Joke: Place this on your enemy's sofa and she'll immediately think her lovely, comfortable new furniture is already broken.

You: What's the difference between my enemy and a bogie?
Enemy: I give up.
You: A bogie only gets up your nose sometimes.

Equipment: A National Lottery ticket.

Joke: Mark up a National Lottery ticket with the winning numbers just after they've been announced and then leave the ticket lying around your enemy's house.

You: Why does my enemy hate alphabet soup?

Enemy: I give up.

You: Because he's bored of always having to eat his words.

Equipment: A telephone.
Joke: Ring up your enemy and tell them that you're the local DJ and that they're now broadcasting live on local radio.

You: What's the difference between the school bully and Winnie the Pooh?
Enemy: I give up.
You: Nothing - they both have very little brain.

Equipment: An enemy.

Joke: When your enemy comes home, tell him that someone called Mr Bailiff called around to see him.

You: What did the new-born baby say to the naughty schoolgirl?

Enemy: I give up.

You: Grow up.

Equipment: Some scouring pads and brown paint
Joke: Wait till your enemy's on a diet and then replace all his crackers with painted scouring pads. But tell him almost immediately.

You: Why did nobody want to sit next to my enemy on the roller coaster?
Enemy: I give up.
You: Because she's always falling out with people.

Equipment: Some false teeth.
Joke: Leave a false tooth in the toothpaste mug so that when your enemy goes to rinse out their teeth, they immediately think their tooth has fallen out.

You: Why was my enemy sitting under a pile of furniture?
Enemy: I give up.
You: Because someone had turned the tables on him.

Equipment: Some clumps of black cotton.

Joke: Leave these on your enemy's hairbrush so that when they brush their hair, they immediately think they're going bald.

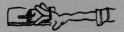

You: What's the difference between my enemy and dandruff?

Enemy: I give up.

You: Nothing - they both get in everyone's hair.

Equipment: A sticker of a spider.
Joke: Stick this on the lens of your enemy's camera.

You: Why is my enemy's brain in perfect condition?
Enemy: I give up.
You: Because it's hardly ever been used.

Equipment: Some sand.
Joke: Just before your enemy gets into a nice, hot bath, pour a layer of sand into the tub so that when they sit down, it's all crunchy.

You: Why did I get hiccups when I swallowed the book about the Romans?
Enemy: I give up.
You: It was just history repeating itself.

Equipment: A packet of flour.
Joke: Empty the contents of your enemy's talcum powder packet and replace them with flour.

You: Why did the class idiot swallow a bottle of bleach?
Enemy: I give up.
You: He was preparing for a stiff exam.

Equipment: A packet of flour.
Joke: Sprinkle some flour into the bottom of your enemy's coat pockets and wait for her to stuff her hands into her pockets and then rub her eyes.

You: Why do gnomes never get hurt in a fight?
Enemy: I give up.
You: They took the elf-defense course.

Equipment: Some foreign coins.
Joke: Secretly empty the contents of your enemy's purse; fill it with foreign coins and then follow him into the local candy store. But carefully keep the real coins nearby.

You: Why did the terrapin get told off?
Enemy: I give up.
You: Because he was turtle-y out of order.